The Original

Climbing
Mt. Whitney

Wynne Benti and Walt Wheelock

with UP THE EAST FACE by Norman Clyde

**SPOTTED
DOG PRESS**®

BISHOP, CALIFORNIA

Climbing Mt. Whitney
©1998, 2000 Wynne Benti, revised edition

Published exclusively by Spotted Dog Press, Inc., Bishop, California
Spotted Dog Press is a registered trademark of Spotted Dog Press, Inc.

**SPOTTED
DOG PRESS**®

WWW.SPOTTEDDOGPRESS.COM

We like to hear from our readers. If you have comments about this book
or others by Spotted Dog Press, please write us at:
Spotted Dog Press
P.O. Box 1721
Bishop CA 93515

Cover photo:
East Face of Mt. Whitney from Russell-Carillon Pass by Edward M. Zdon
Page four:
Mt. Whitney from the summit of Mt. Russell by Pete Yamagata
Maps, book design, and layout by Spotted Dog Press, Inc.
First printing 1997
Revised edition first printing 1998
Revised edition second printing 2001
ISBN Number: 1-893343-00-6
Library of Congress Catalog Number:
97-91533
Printed in the United States of America

A Word About Climbing

Various aspects of hiking, which include climbing mountains, have certain risks and hazards associated with them. Some of these hazards include, but are not limited to, adverse weather conditions, loose rock, exposed rock, rugged terrain, stream crossings, insect or snake bites, hypothermia, heat exhaustion, dehydration, mountain sickness or other types of physical injury which could be lethal.

A book or map is not a substitute for experience, skill, and knowledge of safety procedures. At the time of this writing, route descriptions were accurate, however the authors and publisher of this guide make no representations as to the safety of any hiking or driving route described in this guide. Conditions are constantly changing and it is recommended that you contact the supervising park agency or consult available map information to find out about current conditions. The responsibility for your decisions and actions is yours alone.

"For every climber who blazes a new trail to the unknown heights of Asia and Alaska there will be thousands who follow the familiar routes up familiar peaks — to the summits of the Alps, the Rockies, the hills of Scotland and New England, wherever mountains rise high and challenging above valleys. Their names will not be printed in newspapers or alpine journals. But they too will know discovery and adventure; and they will be no less mountaineers because the peaks they climb have been climbed and conquered before."

James Ramsey Ullman
High Conquest — The Story of Mountaineering

Mt. Whitney from the summit of Mt. Russell

A c k n o w l e d g e m e n t s

We would like to thank the following individuals and organizations for their contributions to this edition of *Climbing Mt. Whitney:* Diana Pietrasanta, Wilderness Manager, Inyo National Forest, Mt. Whitney Ranger Station; the Eastern Sierra Interpretive Association in Bishop; Bill Michael, Director of the Eastern California Museum, County of Inyo and staff for photographs; Nancy Smith of Inyo County Search & Rescue; Dee Molenaar for his illustration of the East Face; Steve Boster, China Lake Naval Air Weapons Station, for aerial photography; the Mt. Whitney Ranger District of the United States Forest Service for providing current trail materials; the Eastern Sierra Interagency Visitor Center in Lone Pine; the Bancroft Library, University of California at Berkeley; Kathleen Hession, R.J. Secor, Gary Vallé, Pete Yamagata and Murray Zichlinsky for their photography; Ed M. Zdon, the younger, for technical route information and photography; Ed Zdon, the elder, for fourteener fashion hints; Ella Power Wheelock, Walt's companion for thirty years, and dedicated lover of the southwest; and finally, Andy Zdon, husband and geologist extraordinaire.

Table of Contents

Good Climbing

Some peaks belong to climbers. Some peaks belong to everyone. In this latter group are such peaks as Mt. Fuji.

Mt. Whitney is coming into this class. Climbers who never before started up the trail are doing so on Mt. Whitney, and doing so successfully. On the otherhand, Whitney provides a challenge to the most skilled mountaineer with its great East Face.

Here we have brought you the story of this great mountain, and the way to climb it, the easy way or the hardest way.

We wish to thank the late Tom Condon, John and Ruth Mendenhall for their advice and assistance on the East Face. John, together with Ruth, climbed all of the routes, and pioneered several. They were the outstanding authorities on Mt. Whitney.

Walt Wheelock

F o r e w o r d
By Wynne Benti

Once, while browsing the book section of a local mountaineering shop, I discovered a collection of rainbow-colored climbing and jeep trail guides with wildly bright covers in shocking pink, chartreuse, and purple. Tucked away in the shadows of a lower shelf, these books were my first introduction to a press named *La Siesta* and its publisher, Walt Wheelock. For some thirty years, Walt quietly published a vast range of titles from the bright yellow *Desert Peaks I* to an equally bright purple book called *Climbing Mt. Whitney*. The simple typewritten pages brought to mind images of peaceful campfires beneath vast starry skies on pinyon-covered ridges; the remains of a ghost town scratched from a desert mountainside; a high Sierra trail, long and winding, through Lodgepole and Columbine to the Arctic-like tundra above timberline.

There were descriptions of routes up peaks in California, not quite as famous as Mt. Whitney, but with colorful names like Crater Mountain, Sage Hen Peak, French Madam and "Hell-Broke-Loose Mountain," Sierra mountaineer and desert climber, Chester Versteeg's affectionate epithet for Volcano Peak in Little Lake Basin, north of Ridgecrest. Simple route descriptions, no more than a paragraph or two, enticed the reader to take the challenge.

My own autumn dayhike up Mt. Whitney started at dawn with a good friend, each lugging a gallon of water up the trail in our daypacks. From sunrise to sunset, our journey from sage to tundra was topped by a cloudless, turquoise-blue sky. Along the beautifully engineered USFS trail, we saw people of all different skill levels in various states of preparedness. Some were decked out in their Sunday best while others were outfitted from head to toe in the latest climbing gear. When we reached Trail Crest at the top of the relentless ninety-seven switchbacks, we knew the summit of Mt. Whitney was easily within our reach. For the first time on the trail, the west side of the Sierra across the Great Western Divide came into view, and it was spectacular. Beyond the imposing red and black ridges of the Kaweahs, miles and miles of rugged granitic terrain stretched across the horizon, speckled with small blue-green lakes, glistening snowfields and impressive knife-edged ridges. About a mile from the summit, my water bottles were empty so I filled them at a creamy-watered seep just off the main trail. In 1991, I met the man who would be my coauthor on *Climbing Mt. Whitney* when I photographed him for an article in a climbing newsletter. During the thirty years that Walt ran his one-man publishing operation, he published more than sixty books on the west, ranging in subject from riverboating on the Sacramento Delta, to exploring the beaches of Baja, and trekking in Nepal. Walt hand-typed each book on a manual typewriter, counting the characters in each line of type for perfect justification to the right and left margins. Proofreading was done the old-fashioned way, without the benefit of spell-checkers and word processing programs. He pasted the typewritten galleys to separate sheets of paper with rubber cement, then picked a color cover stock and had the printer mix one ink color, with a little varnish, to give each book cover some shine. In those days, when stores welcomed small publishers on their doorsteps, Walt sold his books to customers from the trunk of his car.

A year later, I met up with Walt again on a four-wheel drive trip to the ghost towns of Masonic, Bodie, and Aurora, and it was on this trip that you might say, we bonded. With him was Ella Power, his companion of more than 30 years. The changes that the two of them had seen during the 20th century was awesome, certainly from a historical perspective. They each grew up in a west that saw the transition from horse to horseless carriage, from dirt to paved roads, from orange groves to sprawling residential developments — he, from Oregon to Glendale; she from Phoenix, Arizona to Monterey Park.

During the warm harvest moon evenings in Glendale, we listened to Walt's stories while he filled our glasses with a thick gold-flaked liqueur from Baja. With his trademark stone white hair and beard, he reminded one of an eccentric Albert Einstein. He talked about the "good old days" — adventures in his beloved Baja, the friends and loves of his life. He spent weekends with Francis Farquhar (*History of the Sierra Nevada*) at his Berkeley home, visited with photographer Ansel Adams and entertained Horace Albright, the Director of the National Park Service. Walt also loved women and they loved him.

There were three wives, two daughters, and numerous romances with women across the west. Each was a cherished character in the story of his life — and he had outlived almost all of them.

Two years before the stock market crash of 1929, Walt traveled with his high school class in Model T's to Death Valley. Back then, it took almost two days to get to Death Valley from Los Angeles. The paved highway ended in Mojave where an old wagon route was followed north. On the way, they spent a night camped on the concrete foundation of a new bank under construction in the high-desert town of Johannesburg. Walt recalled, "Four kids could lift a Model T out of the sand if it got stuck, but we never got stuck."

In 1935, Walt received the first degree in Astronomy ever granted by UCLA. He once said, "When I got out of school during the depression, I couldn't even get a job sweeping out an observatory." Instead, he found a job as a foot patrolman on the night beat in Glendale, which required checking the doors of downtown Glendale shops to make sure they were locked. He wrote a number of articles on astronomy which were published by the Astronomical Society of America and the Mt. Wilson Observatory Group. In 1927, he climbed his first peak, Mt. Wilson, by hiking up the front range of the San Gabriels from Pasadena.

Walt worked with many different authors who played a role in recording the history of the eastern Sierra Nevada, Death Valley, and the Great Basin — a list which included Norman Clyde, Mary DeDecker, L. Burr Belden, and Ardis M. Walker. The great Sierra mountaineer Norman Clyde, who wrote *Close Ups of the High Sierra* (published by Spotted Dog Press) was credited with over a thousand first ascents in the Sierra Nevada.

Climbing Mt. Whitney was Walt's last book. Six months after the first edition was published in 1997, he collapsed while working in his garden. He fell into a coma from which he never awoke, and died a week later.

If there is a place to go when we leave this physical world, Walt Wheelock is there now, holding a martini and sharing a laugh with his old cronies, above the hawks and the hang-gliders, where the clouds roll off the mountaintops and the setting sun paints the sky red.

July 6, 1864

At last I reached the top, and, with the greatest caution, wormed my body over the brink, and rolling out upon the smooth surface of the granite, looked over and watched Cotter make his climb.

He came steadily up, with no sense of nervousness, until he got to the narrow part of the ice, and here he stopped and looked up with a forlorn face to me; and he asked if it had occurred to me that we had, by and by, to go down again.

We had now an easy slope to the summit, and hurried up over rocks and ice, reaching the crest at exactly twelve o'clock.

I rang my hammer upon the topmost rock; we grasped hands, and I reverently named the grand peak Mount Tyndall.

To our surprise, upon sweeping the horizon with my level, there appeared two peaks equal in height with us, and two rising even higher. That which looked highest of all was a cleanly cut helmet of granite upon the same ridge with Mount Tyndall, lying about six miles south, and fronting the desert with a bold square bluff which rises to the crest of the peak, where a white fold of snow trims it gracefully.

Mount Whitney, as we afterwards called it in honor of our chief, is probably the highest land within the United States. Its summit looked glorious, but inaccessible.

Clarence King
Mountaineering in the Sierra Nevada

Illustration by Dee Molenaar

Mt. Whitney from the Owens Valley. Photo: Bill Fettkether, courtesy China Lake NAWS

C   H   A   P   T   E   R   O   N   E

The Story of Whitney

Whitney is a shy mountain. The fire peaks of the Cascades proudly hold up their snowcapped crowns for all to admire, while Mt. Whitney ordinarily may only be viewed from the east over closer and more apparent peaks. From the San Joaquin Valley, Mt. Whitney is completely hidden. As a result, Shasta was known in 1788, Hood and Rainier in 1792. Seventy years later, the existence of the highest mountain in the United States was still unsuspected.

The first white man to leave a record of this area was the trapper Joseph Reddeford Walker. After wintering in the San Joaquin Valley, he started east on February 14, 1834. He crossed the Sierra Nevada via Walker Pass. Working north through the Owens Valley, he turned east through Montgomery Pass. If Walker noticed Mt. Whitney among the cluster of peaks west of Owens Lake, he made no mention of it. To the early explorers, the passes, not the peaks were the important features.

With the influx of miners during the Gold Rush days, many moved into the foothills, but the high mountains remained unexplored. Many believed that all of the placer gold, found in the lowland stream beds had come from a "mother lode" somewhere back in the high country. In 1860, the California State Legislature authorized the formation of the California State Geological Survey, appointing Josiah Dwight Whitney as the state geologist. The survey was to prepare a geological, botanical and zoological history of the state and "to examine for gold, silver, and copper." The Survey began its field work on December 12, and the year of 1861 was spent exploring the Coast Ranges, mostly in Southern California. During 1862, the Survey moved north, highlighting that year's work with an ascent of Mount Shasta.

Professor William H. Brewer, from Yale University, was in charge of the field party and his letters to friends at Yale fired the enthusiasm of a recent graduate, Clarence King. In 1863, King, together with James Gardiner, a fellow graduate of Yale's Sheffield Scientific School, started

The Whitney Survey Field Party of 1864: Gardiner, Cotter, Brewer and King
The Bancroft Library, University of California, Berkeley

west across the plains and mountains.

On arriving in California, King and Gardiner had the luck to find that Brewer was journeying to San Francisco on the same steamer on which they had taken passage. King introduced himself, and by the time the boat had reached the San Francisco Bay, had impressed Brewer with his ability. The following day, Brewer introduced the pair to Professor Whitney and the two were engaged as "volunteer assistants." They added in some exploration in the southern High Sierra during the remainder of that year. The following year, the party worked its way toward the headwaters of the South Fork of the Kings River. On July 2, 1864, Brewer and his topographer, Hoffman, climbed a fine peak, just east of their camp. Brewer wrote in his journal:

"We were not on the highest peak, although we were a thousand feet higher than we anticipated any peaks were. We had not supposed there were any over 12,000 or 12,500, while we were actually up over 13,600, and there were a dozen peaks in sight as high or higher." The party named the peak Mount Brewer.

When the climbers returned to camp and told of the startling array of high peaks, excitement grew. Of all of the party, King was the most insistent that an attempt should be made to reach the highest summit. Brewer wrote:

"King is enthusiastic, is wonderfully tough, has the greatest endurance I have ever seen, and is withal very muscular." Dick Cotter, a packer, agreed to accompany him. On July 4, with Brewer and Gardiner carrying their forty pound packs to the first dividing ridge, King and Cotter started their climb. The adventure is told, and perhaps heightened a bit in King's *Mountaineering in the Sierra Nevada*. The story of cannonading rocks and hair-raising cornices seem strange to modern climbers, but it must be remembered that mountain-climbing was an unusual activity in the United States in 1864, and the two were crossing the Sierra with no knowledge of ridges or watersheds. As Brewer wrote:

"It's easy enough to climb a mountain when you know where to go."

On July 6, the two stood on top of what had appeared to be the highest summit. To their amazement, two peaks were higher. The highest was named Mt. Whitney for their chief, since they were sure it was the highest point in the United States. Food was running low, their clothes were in tatters and Cotter's shoes were falling apart. There was nothing to do but return, with Cotter's feet wrapped in strips of blanket.

As supplies in camp were also low, Brewer and King returned to Visalia. All the way, King pleaded for another chance. Brewer finally consented and gave him an escort of two cavalrymen, a pack horse and rations for two weeks. On July 14, he rode up the South Fork of the Kaweah River on the newly constructed Hockett Trail.

The party crossed the Great Western Divide, dropped to the Kern River, and finally climbed onto the Kern Plateau. They worked east, following a canyon to the north of what King had named Sheep Rock (Mt. Langley, 14,042'). He had chosen a poor route, too far to the east, and was stopped by a sheer cliff, some four hundred feet from the top. In the geological report, *Geology*, by the Whitney Survey, King wrote:

"Mt. Whitney is a ridge having somewhat the outline of a helmet, the perpendicular face being turned toward the east. There is snow on its summit, which indicates there must be a flat surface there. The mountain is the culminating point of an immense pile of granite, which

First to climb Mt. Whitney: Lone Pine residents Charles D. Begole, Albert H. Johnson and John Lucas (not pictured)
Photos: Eastern California Museum Collection

is cut almost to the center by numerous steep and vertical canyons… This mountain has been approached from all sides, except the east, and found to be absolutely inaccessible." The rest of that year and the following year were spent in the Yosemite region and with this, King completed his work with the Survey.

In 1867, King was appointed U.S. Geologist in charge of the Geological Exploration of the Fortieth Parallel, the forebear of the United States Geological Survey. Most of this work was through Nevada and Utah and it was not until 1871 that King was to find an excuse to check the east slope of the Sierra Nevada, again to take up the challenge of Mt. Whitney. Leaving Carson City, he took the stage to Lone Pine and engaged a Frenchman, Paul Pinson, to accompany him. That evening, looking up through the storm clouds that partly obscured the Sierra, he gazed at "the sharp terrible crest of Whitney, still red with the reflected light from the long sunken sun."

King's account of his ascent tells of precipices and treacherous ice crests, till finally:

"Above us, but thirty feet rose to a crest, beyond which we saw nothing. I dared not think it the summit, till we stood there, and Mt. Whitney was under our feet."

Clouds obscured the view to the north where the true Mt. Whitney lay. King took a barometric altitude and found it some five hundred feet lower than he had expected it to be, but blamed it on the severe Sierra storm.

Two years later, W.A. Goodyear, a former member of the State Geological Survey, sent this to the California Academy of Sciences:

"On the 27th day of July 1873, Mr. M.W. Belshaw of Cerro Gordo, and myself, rode our mules to the highest crest of a peak southwest of

The Smithsonian summit shelter on Mt. Whitney, early 1900's. Pictured (l to r) are Owens Valley residents William Parcher, William Chalfant, unknown, Burton Frasher, Sr and unknown.
Photo: Burton Frasher, Eastern California Museum Collection

Lone Pine which, for over three years has been known by the name of Mt. Whitney, and which was measured and ascended as such by Mr. Clarence King, in the summer of 1871… It is by no means the highest of the grand cluster of peaks which form the culminating portion of the Sierra Nevada; nor is it the peak which was discovered by Professor W. H. Brewer and party, in 1864, and originally named by them Mount Whitney."

King read this in the Academy's proceedings, and admitted the accuracy of Goodyear's remarks. He hastened west and on September 19, 1873, King at long last stood on the summit of Mt. Whitney. Unfortunately for King, two parties preceded him. Unfortunately for our historians, these parties at the time of their climbs, had not taken them seriously, and had failed to document their claims.

After King's ascent a great controversy arose, the first two parties vying for the honor of the first ascent, and one of them, a group of fishermen, wishing to place the name "Fisherman's Peak" on the summit. The following is the generally accepted list of climbs for 1873:

1. August 18: Charles D. Begole, Albert H. Johnson and John Lucas, "The Fishermen," all residents of Lone Pine. Generally accepted as the first ascent.

2. Date uncertain: William Crapo and Abe Leyda. Crapo claimed

a first ascent with Leyda of August 15, but the argument is not convincing. It seems likely that the date of this ascent was after August 20.

3. September 6: William L. Hunter, Carl Rabe, William Crapo and Tom McDonough
4. September 19: Clarence King and Frank Knowles
5. October 21: John Muir, via what is now known as the Mountaineer's Route.

No ascent was recorded in 1874. The following year saw increasing activity. A party of nine made the climb on October 3, and one of the party, Professor W.E. James, took sixteen photographs on the summit. The Wheeler Survey put two parties on top the same fall. In 1878, the first ascent by a woman was made when a party from Porterville climbed Whitney. Four of the group were women. They were Mrs. R.C. Redd, Hope Broughton, Mary Martin, and Anna Mills.

The first of many scientific expeditions was that of Professor Samuel Langley in 1881. As a result, the U.S. Army proclaimed the region a military reservation for the use of the Signal Corps, the weather bureau at the time. In 1901, it was returned to the Sierra Forest Reserve. In 1903, Professor Alexander G. McAdie visited the summit with a Sierra Club group of 103 climbers. Professor McAdie strongly recommended the use of the mountain for meteorological observations.

The route was considered too hazardous for stock animals, so the people of Lone Pine raised funds to build a horse trail. G.E. Marsh completed the trail on July 22, 1904. Four days later, three workmen were knocked down by a lightening bolt, with one fatality.

The Smithsonian Institute became interested in Whitney as a location for the study of solar radiation. In the meantime, the trail had fallen into disrepair. The citizens of Lone Pine once again raised funds for the new trail and on August 27, announced the finishing of the summit shelter that still stands, just below the highest point.

After World War II, the Forest Service undertook to realign the trail and wrangled a large air compressor to near the 12,500 foot level. With its aid, an excellent trail was blasted from the rocky buttress, bypassing the snow fields that often blocked the old trail until late summer.

"The supreme joy I felt when I realized that my prayer had been answered, and that I was at last really standing on the summit of Mt. Whitney, knew no bounds. For the time being I forgot that I was ever tired; one glance was enough to compensate for all the trials of the trip. How strange it seemed to be looking off for a distance of seventy miles down into Death Valley, the lowest point...Oh what an inspiration it was to look from that magnificent peak on the grand panorama of mountains, reaching from beyond the Yosemite to San Bernardino! Range after range in every direction, peak on peak, comprising almost limitless forms, rise one above the other, each striving for the mastery."

Anna Mills, one of the four first women to climb Mt. Whitney, 1878

Women climbers at the summit cairn on Mt. Whitney, circa 1880.
Photo: Eastern California Museum

Geology

During the early Paleozoic Era, 550 to 410 million years ago, the area that is now the Sierra Nevada was covered by seawater. Marine sedimentary rocks were deposited during this time, and remnants of these ancient rocks are still present in the Sierra Nevada to the north of Mt. Whitney.

Approximately 400 million years ago, collisions between the North American Plate, and its neighboring plate resulted in folding and faulting of the marine rocks deposited earlier. This event is called the Antler orogeny, orogeny being a geologic term for an episode of mountain building. The Antler orogeny resulted in the development of a mountain chain east of the present Sierra Nevada. During the following 25 million years of subsidence and erosion, the Antler Mountains eroded away and a new ocean basin formed.

The Late Permian and Early Triassic periods, approximately 250 to 350 million years ago, were marked by a collision which occurred between the North American Plate and one or more of its neighbors. This event, which occurred at a time when dinosaurs were becoming a dominant life form, is termed the Sonoma orogeny. The Sonoma orogeny further deformed the existing rocks in the area and caused regional uplift in central Nevada. Basins formed on either side of this uplift, including the area of the present day Sierra Nevada. The stage was now set for a great mountain building event.

About 220 to 215 million years ago, the North American Plate changed direction forcing the adjacent oceanic plate to the west to get shoved or "subducted" beneath the North American Plate. This caused volcanism in the region.

The Whitney Crest Photo: Norman Clyde, Eastern California Museum Collection

Following a five million year period of relative inactivity, further collision occurred during the Jurassic Period, about 210 million years ago. Tear-dropped shaped bodies of molten rock called "plutons" ascended through the crust due to their light density. These plutons shoved aside the existing rock, and as they reached the surface, crystallized due to decreasing heat and pressure. The greatest period of emplacement of these plutons was during the late Jurassic and Cretaceous Periods, 210 to 80 million years ago. These are the granitic rocks we see throughout the Sierra Nevada today. Mountain building occurred along with the plutonic emplacement and this event is termed the Nevadan orogeny. An ancestral mountain range in the area of the present-day Sierra Nevada had been built.

As the Nevadan orogeny winded down and ended, erosion began to occur in the Sierra Nevada region. The Nevadan mountains eventually eroded to a chain of gently rolling hills, probably much similar in appearance to the present-day foothills of the Sierra Nevada to the west.

Then about 30 million years ago, renewed uplift began to occur in the Sierra Nevada region. By 20 million years ago, the Sierra Nevada had tilted to the west. Volcanism occurred in the Sierra Nevada to the north. About three million years ago, major uplift of the Sierra Nevada began, resulting in the massive escarpment along the Sierra Nevada that we see today. At the present time, uplift continues and was dramatically displayed during the 1872 Owens Valley earthquake. It is thought that the Sierra Nevada uplifted at least six feet in elevation.

As the surface was lifted, drainage to the west and the east led to stream erosion, forming the great canyons of the Sierra. In the Whitney region, a long north-south faultline, west of the summit ridge disrupted the stream formation and the westerly streams from the crest found it easier to follow the fault to the south, forming Kern River Canyon. Following the last uplift and continuing until the past 10,000 years was the planing of the ice-age glaciers, changing the V-shaped river canyons to the present U-shaped glacial canyons. This is quite noticeable in upper Lone Pine Canyon. The piles of rubble (moraines) may be seen near Whitney Portal. Glaciers do not carve out a single smooth slope, but due to the quarrying effect caused by the fracture of granite blocks, scoop out steps or benches. Whitney Portal, Lone Pine Lake, Whitney Outpost, and Mirror Lake are examples of such glacial scoops. An amazing feature of Mt. Whitney's summit is remnant land surface left over from the gently rolling hills that were first uplifted about 30 million years ago.

Rock

The igneous rocks may be divided into two large groups, the acidic or light colored rocks (light both in color and weight) and the basic or dark-colored rocks. Basalt, of which the great lava flows near Little Lake are composed, is the most common basic rock.

The light rocks vary greatly in appearance. If the molten magma is suddenly cooled, crystals are not formed and the rock becomes volcanic glass or obsidian. If the cooling is a little slower, microscopic crystals are formed and we have rhyolite. In normal cooling beneath the surface, the crystals are 0.1 to 0.2 inches long and the rock is granite. If the cooling is still slower, much larger crystals appear in the rock, and it then carries the additional title of porphyry. Yet all of these rocks have the same chemical composition. In general, granite consists of quartz, feldspar, micas, and small amounts of other minerals such as garnet. If quartz is missing, the rock is called monzonite. If a little quartz is present, it becomes quartz monzonite. It is of these monzonites that

Looking across Mt. Whitney from the west to the Inyo Mountains. Photo: China Lake NAWS

Mt. Whitney is formed. It is the feldspar in these rocks that gives Mt. Whitney its very notable pinkish-white appearance which is so striking in the light of the setting sun.

Mt. Whitney Communities

Elevation	Community	Life Zone
14,000'	Alpine	Arctic-Alpine
	Subalpine Forest	Hudsonian
10,000'	Lodgepole-Red Fir Forest	Canadian
	Yellow Pine Forest	Transition
		Upper Sonoran
	Desert Chaparral	
	Lower Chaparral	
		Lower Sonoran
	Alkali Sink Creosote Bush Sagebrush Scrub	
3,000'		

C H A P T E R   T H R E E

Flora & Fauna

The types of plants and animals found in the Whitney region can be classified by changes in climate and elevation. As a comparison, we find that as we travel north from the equator, or up from sea level, the climate becomes colder. Roughly speaking, a rise in elevation of 1,000 feet is equivalent to a northward journey, across latitudes, of 300 miles. From Owens Lake in the deepest valley to the summit of Mt. Whitney is a gain of almost 11,000 feet, representing a climatic change equivalent to what one would find traveling the distance between Mazatlan, Mexico and Nome, Alaska.

In the late nineteenth century, C. Hart Merriam developed the life zone system for classifying vegetation based on climatic data found in changes of elevation and latitude. The life zone system, which has been used for decades since its initial development, was a way to describe any given geographic area based on vegetation type and the amount of precipitation (rainfall) the area in question received. Each life zone was named after a geographical area which had temperatures similar to those areas observed by Merriam as he traveled from the bottom of Grand Canyon (Lower Sonoran life zone) to the tops of the San Francisco Peaks (Arctic-Alpine life zone) outside of Flagstaff, Arizona. Merriam's life zone system made the connection between elevation and latitude, but because it was based on climate – temperature and precipitation – it's relevance was applicable to only the American southwest.

In the decades following Merriam's concept of life zones, several other systems for identifying plant communities were proposed and put into use. One of these was the concept of biomes, proposed by ecologists Frederic Clements and Victor Shelford shortly before World War II. A biome was described as an ecosystem where differences in temperature and precipitation created a unique community of plants and animals. In 1959, Philip Munz and David Keck developed the classification system of plant communities, a very broad system of classification essentially based on the dominant plant species that occupy any given area. This system has achieved a great deal of popularity and is the one currently preferred by California ecologists.

Lone Pine Creek flows from snow banks high on the Sierra crest in the Arctic-Alpine life zone or Alpine community, until the waters sink into the desert sands in the Lower Sonoran life zone or Sagebrush Scrub community. All of this takes place in some fifteen miles. At Lone Pine, the Lower Sonoran life zone, we have the Black-tailed Jackrabbit living in the shade of the Creosote bushes and the yellow-flowered Rabbit Brush. As the roadway enters Lone Pine Canyon, the desert Juniper and Pinyon Pine are found, along with mule deer. By the time we reach the end of the road and the beginning of the Mt. Whitney trail, we have journeyed into the northern United States with Jeffrey Pines and Red Firs shading a tumbling trout stream and small woodland tarn.

Shortly above here, White Fir and Lodgepole Pine take over as we pass into the Canadian life zone or Lodgepole-Red Fir Forest community. Beyond this, Mountain Hemlock, with its unique horizontal branches, replaces the White Fir. By the time we reach Mirror Lake, we are well into the Hudsonian life zone or Subalpine Forest community, with the Lodgepole Pine only growing in sheltered places. Soon thereafter, we reach the White Pine region, and by the time the Consultation Lake junction is reached, only the White-bark Pine remains, and the Albicaulis, hugging the ground and growing but a few inches a year. Above this point, a few shrubs struggle, and finally, the only "tree" left is the Alpine Willow which grows to the magnificent height of just four inches.

The animals, being more mobile, range higher during the sand so we find them high among the rocks along the trail. A large woodchuck, the Yellow-Bellied Marmot, is the largest of the alpine animals. His sharp whistle may startle you as he announces your arrival in his domain. Often he will respond and carry on a "conversation" with you, if you return his friendly whistle. Still higher is found the Pika or

Lone Pine Lake. Photo: Kathleen Hession

Cony, resembling a small gray short-eared rabbit, but only some seven inches in length. He sounds off with a clicking noise, something like the tone of two rocks being sharply struck together. Often he will freeze, as he watches you, in an upright position (giving him his nick-name of "picket-pin").

But even on the summit of Whitney, in the Arctic-Alpine life zone or Alpine community, down among the cracks between the rocks, we find delightful wildflower gardens, with the blooms holding their heads maybe an inch off the ground. And with these flowers will be the summer insects buzzing around, gathering their honey.

However, as we climb the trail, we are forced to realize that the life zones are not so neatly cut. Lone Pine Canyon is an excellent place to observe "micro-climates," small patches that differ from the surrounding plant growth, as under the shade of an oak tree, we find flowers blooming, while the surrounding meadow grasses have already turned brown. In the lower canyon, a long tongue of aspen and pines extends far down along the creek bed into the Pinyon-Juniper community. At Whitney Portal, the pines and firs form a complete stand, while half a mile further up the trail, we pass into a chaparral-covered slope, void of any trees, where the sun shines so brightly, as the climbers so well know on a hot day.

But at the same level, a few yards to the left, under the shading cliffs of Mt. Candlelight (12,000'+), the conifers extend along the stream bed. Many a hiker has looked longingly at the deep shade of the pines, as he struggles in the heat and dust, just a few feet away.

So the alert climber has an unexcelled opportunity to study the entire series of life zones of the northern hemisphere in the short distance from Highways 395 to the Whitney Crest.

Lone Pine Creek and its many lakes provide excellent fishing, in spite of the heavy usage they receive. The North Fork and the higher lakes, Consultation and Iceberg (also known as East Face Lake on some maps), are more remote and are more likely to produce a good catch.

The Golden Trout, the state fish of California, has sometimes been called the Mt. Whitney trout. First discovered in the headwaters of the South Fork of the Kern River, it was introduced into the Cottonwood Lakes in 1893. Since that time, it has been planted in many of the high lakes of the Sierra. A close relative, the Rainbow Trout, also a California native, has likewise been widely planted in this area, and the two have interbred so that all shades from golden to white may now be taken.

The Mt. Whitney Hatchery, near Independence, has cultured these, as well as the Eastern Brook and the Brown Trout. The streams and lakes of Whitney are stocked throughout the year with fish.

C H A P T E R   F O U R

Gear & Food

Norman Clyde, the great California mountaineer who made more than fifty ascents of Mt. Whitney from every possible route and angle, was famous for carrying a pack that weighed over a hundred pounds. Among the items he carried were a large cast iron skillet for frying up fresh trout, a fishing rod, a cobbler's kit for repairing the nails on his "hobnailed" hiking boots, a firearm of some sort for hunting, a full size axe — you get the picture. Lightweight stoves have since replaced the iron skillet; the one-person bivy sack has replaced the two-person tent, and tube-fed neoprene water pouches worn on the back have replaced conventional water bottles.

The Ten Essentials

Mt. Whitney has been climbed by hikers in all types of clothing and as many types of footgear. Bikinis and low tennis shoes have been worn, but chances of success are greater with clothing designed for outdoor survival — synthetic fibers, nylon, pile and polypropylene. Though Sierra summer days may start out sunny and beautiful without a cloud in the sky, by early afternoon, thunderheads may be building up across the crest. If trapped by a sudden Sierra storm, it is not your comfort, but possibly your life that may be at stake. Every daypack or backpack should contain the following list of items, commonly referred to as the ten essentials:

- Map
- Compass
- Flashlight or headlamp, spare batteries
- Water with electrolyte replacement powder and energy food/snacks
- Clothing. Dress in layers. Include lightweight rain jacket/pants that can also double as a windbreaker; lightweight polypropylene or other synthetic underwear – tops and bottoms; synthetic or wool sweater
- Pocket knife
- Matches in waterproof container or plastic baggie
- Sunglasses, sunscreen
- Hat
- First aid kit
  Additional equipment is discussed below in greater detail.

Clothing

From June 15 to September 15, the climate of Mt. Whitney is usually mild, clear and sunny. There are years when the "Class 1" (the standard Whitney Trail up from Whitney Portal is rated Class 1 — easy, trail walking— on the Yosemite Decimal System) climbing season doesn't begin until well into July due to a late snow year. 1998, the year of "El Niño," was a very late snow year.

Clothing is more often needed for protection from the sun than from the cold. Your sea-level tan is little protection against the ultraviolet light present at 14,000 feet. The best way to dress for any backcountry trip is in "layers" since the weather can change dramatically. Layers of clothing can be added or removed as conditions change. A warm Sierra morning, where a tee-shirt and shorts are perfect gear, can by afternoon turn into a cold, downpour requiring a sweater, rain jacket and rain pants.

A light, long-sleeved shirt, long pants or shorts, a brimmed hat and a good pair of UV blocking sunglasses make up the usual clothing. Sunscreen should be carried for face and lips. If you wear a tee-shirt and shorts, it's a good idea to carry a pair of lightweight synthetic underwear, a long-sleeve top and bottoms, as well as a lightweight rain jacket and a pair of rain pants. When traveling in the Sierra backcountry,

Septuagenarian Ed Zdon models the latest in sleepwear & slippers at Outpost Camp.
Photo: Andy Zdon

raingear is an essential item to have in your daypack or backpack. Also carry a synthetic or wool sweater or lightweight down parka. Wool and synthetic fibers dry more quickly than cotton and are better insulators if wet. Cotton materials, on the otherhand, hold in moisture when wet and are almost impossible to dry out without the aid of the sun. Most Sierra thunderstorms show up with little or no warning, and during the summer, afternoon storms can be a daily occurence. Dressing in layers with a parka or synthetic sweater covered by a rain jacket and a pair of rain pants will mean the difference between comfort and misery.

Footgear

Care of your feet is really important. This means wearing both adequate shoes and equally adequate socks. Lightweight walking boots or running shoes are popular on dayhikes, but provide little ankle support and are rapidly chewed to pieces over rough terrain. Hiking boots with Vibram or similar heavy-duty soles are the best. A pair of light socks, usually of a synthetic material like polypropylene, and a pair of heavy wool socks, worn over the lighter pair of socks complete the footgear. On overnight trips, carry extra dry, clean socks. Using clean socks and taping potential hotspots with moleskin or waterproof first aid tape before getting on the trail, will help prevent blisters.

Sleeping Bag

A sleeping bag is a must for an overnight trip. Down is the lightest, warmest and most expensive. Synthetic bags are heavier than down, but very satisfactory. Car-camping style sleeping bags, made of Dacron, with canvas exteriors and flannel interiors are too bulky and heavy to carry on an overnight backpacking trip. Add an air mattress or ensolite pad for greater comfort. Bring a lightweight plastic or nylon ground cloth to put beneath your sleeping bag and pad, or your tent. A bivy sack, which slips right over your sleeping bag and provides fairly waterproof, wind resistant coverage, is a lightweight alternative to carrying a tent on overnight trips.

Pack

For overnight trips, an internal or external frame backpack is needed. Years ago, external frame packs were once the pack of choice by most and were about the only style of pack available from any outdoor equipment supply store. Internal frame packs have become very popular because a more compact and weight-balanced load can be carried, allowing for increased speed and greater comfort on the trail.

Tent or Bivy Sack

For overnight trips, consider carrying a tent or bivy sack. Whichever you choose, lightweight is the way to go. There are many two-person tents on the market which are under six pounds. Split the tent up between the hiking partners (one carries the poles and rain-fly while the other carries the tent) to share the weight. Another option, particularly for the solo hiker, is a bivy sack. Bivy sacks weigh less than two pounds, are made of breathable, waterproof nylon, and can withstand a vigorous thunderstorm or other short-term inclement weather. Fairly spacious, they slip right over a sleeping bag and are roomy enough to allow the user to cook a meal and perform other around the camp functions, while enjoying the toasty warmth of the sleeping bag. Bivy sacks alone have provided excellent shelter on unexpected overnight stays on some of the highest peaks in the world.

Almost there — the summit of Mt. Whitney on the final approach from Trail Crest. Photo by Pete Yamagata

Water & Electrolytes

There is no water on the first two miles of the Whitney Trail. There is water on the way to Trail Camp, but due to Giardia infestation, sadly no water in the Sierra should be used without filtering or chemical treatment. Portable water filters, available from outdoor equipment retailers, are typically used on overnight backpacking trips when it's not convenient to carry the additional weight of bottled water. Water can be boiled or treated with iodine crystals, but filtering is considered the most effective way to treat water for Giardia. Dayhikers may want to carry their own water. During summer, it is highly recommended that a minimum of three to four quarts of water be carried. Add to your daypack, a few packets of electrolyte replacement like Gookinaid or Gatorade powder, which can be added to bottled water, to help replenish the body's electrolytes, salts and minerals lost through expiration and perspiration.

Cooking

Campfires are prohibited in the entire Mt. Whitney Zone, so a small backpacking stove is essential, unless you are planning to carry food that doesn't need cooking. This means that you'll be limited to single burner and one-dish meals. It's generally a good idea to cook in a pot that is not going to be used to boil water. There's nothing more unpleasant than drinking a cup of morning coffee which has been prepared in a pot with the after-dinner residues of last night's overcooked seafood jumbalaya. The ideal solution, though more weighty, is to carry two lightweight pots, one for water and one for cooking. One pot for boiling only water, combined with the use of freeze-dried foods or meals that can be cooked in a bag or separate bowl, is a good solution to the additional weight and bulk of two pots. Water can also be used for coffee or some other hot drink. Broth or pre-packaged powdered soups are a good way to rehydrate the body's lost liquids and salts while waiting for dinner to cook. Consider carrying a mix of salty, sweet, and bland foods. At elevation, your physical condition will determine what foods you can eat or what will appeal to you — and they are often not the same cravings you have at lower elevation when packing for the trip. On a nauseous stomach, bland tortillas or saltine crackers and broth may be more appealing than a big dinner. Also carry foods that don't require cooking, like power bars, muffins, bagels, dried fruit, salted pistachios or cashews, trail mix, and smoked jerky.

Food

This is largely a matter of personal preference. Freeze-dried foods are a lightweight, yet somewhat more expensive solution for the dinner meal. Food requires twice as long to cook, each time the altitude is increased by 5,000 feet. Food cooking in ten minutes at sea-level requires 20 minutes at 5,000 feet, 40 minutes at 10,000 feet and over an hour at the 12,000 foot level.

Carry about 8 ounces of protein per person per day: a meat, like smoked jerky, canned chicken, low-fat or fat-free cheese, or nuts; and about 8 ounces of carbohydrates which might include crackers, rolls, cookies, candy. Also include fruit like apples, dried peaches, pineapple (high in potassium), or small cans of fruit cocktail in light syrup. Many people have trouble digesting fats and oils at high altitude. Avoid fried foods, especially on the morning of the summit dash.

Flashlight, First Aid & A Camera

Carry a flashlight or headlamp with extra bulb and batteries. You may not need it, but if you are unexpectedly on the trail after dark it may come in handy. Take a camera with extra film. You will certainly want to record your summit victory. The views from the Whitney Crest and through the "windows" above Trail Crest are ones that can't be duplicated.

A small first aid kit, with moleskin and adhesive tape should be carried. Apply moleskin at the first indication of a blister. Some people will tape their heels with waterproof first aid tape before the hike to help prevent blistering from the onset. Carry aspirin or acetaminophen (the latter is gentler on stomachs) for possible high-altitude headaches and an antacid for nausea. Drinking a lot of water with electrolytes will help minimize the symptoms of dehydration — headaches and nausea.

From late July to the end of September, technical climbing gear is for the most part, not needed on the Whitney Trail. However, from late fall to early summer, depending on conditions (check with the Mt.

Mt. Muir from Trail Camp. Photo by Pete Yamagata

Whitney Ranger District prior to your climb for current conditions), an ice axe and crampons are needed as well as the knowledge on how to use them — this is mountaineering, which requires training and skill. During 1998 (year of the infamous El Niño), ice axes were needed throughout the entire month of July on the Mt. Whitney Trail.

Wilderness Sanitation

The protozoan parasite Giardia Lamblia originates from the contamination of water and food by human and animal waste. With the increased popularity of the Mt. Whitney area, it is important to know a few things about wilderness hygiene that will minimize the health hazard posed by improper disposal of human waste. First, wash hands away from all water sources before eating or preparing food. Use all soaps, even biodegradable ones, as far away from lakes and streams as possible. General rule of thumb, don't wash anything in any body of water. Carry water away from natural sources in a collapsible bucket.

A lightweight plastic trowel should be used to dig a hole about 8"–10" deep to dispose of human waste. Dig your hole at least 100 feet away (40 paces) from any water source. Intestinal pathogens like Giardia and E. Coli can live for years in buried human waste, and thanks to all the folks who don't know how to s - - t in the woods, we have filled our streams and lakes with these nasty bugs.

It is imperative that toilet paper be packed out — ziplock baggies are excellent for this. There is nothing more frustrating then spending all day to get to a scenic spot only to discover piles of rocks with streamers of toilet paper blowing in the wind, or improperly buried toilet paper that has been dug up by some poor animal in search of a meal. Some folks burn and bury it, but entire forests have actually been burned to the ground by this practice, so we don't recommend it.

B.Y.O.T.P. (Bring Your Own Toilet Paper) restrooms have been installed at Outpost and Trail Camp. Since they naturally digest human waste, the USFS asks that trash not be thrown down them, as anything other than organic material and toilet paper interferes with the natural decomposition. The Mt. Whitney Trail is like any other wilderness area — pack out what you bring in — there is no garbage service.

Mountain (Altitude) Sickness

Chances are, if you come up to climb Mt. Whitney from sea level, and aren't use to climbing above 8,000+ feet (though the symptoms of mountain sickness can start at any elevation), you should be prepared for possible discomfort — headache, nausea, dizziness, vomiting — all symptoms of mountain sickness (also called altitude sickness). To minimize your chances of getting sick at elevation, drink a lot of water with electrolyte replacement and eat energy snacks throughout the day. We carry Mylanta for stomach nausea and acetaminophen for headaches (acetaminophen is gentler on nauseated stomachs than conventional aspirin). Some people are just sensitive to elevation and no amount of water or food is going to keep them from getting sick. The key is to be able to judge how you handle high elevation when you are there, and to do something about it for future trips, so that you don't become a liability to your climbing partners or to yourself.

Diamox is a prescription drug which is very effective in relieving the discomforting symptoms associated with mountain sickness, when taken in gradual doses three to four days prior to going to elevation. Simply explained, Diamox functions as a diuretic and helps flush lactic acid out of the body. Lactic acid builds up in the cells as a result of strenuous exercise or activity like mountain climbing, and if the lactic acid isn't flushed out of the body by drinking enough liquid, resulting symptoms can include nausea, vomiting, and headache.

The air is much thinner at 14,000' than at sea level, and the lungs must work much harder for oxygen. Over the years, we have noticed that smokers or people who have smoked heavily in the past, but who have quit, tend to be affected by mountain sickness more often than people who have never smoked.

There are entire books written about the subject by experts in the field of mountain or altitude sickness. Listed below are a few books for further reading on the subject:

High Altitude Illness and Wellness by Charles Houston, M.D.

Mountain Sickness: Prevention, Recognition and Treatment
    by Peter Hackett, M.D.

Mountain Medicine and Physiology: Proceedings of a Symposium for Mountaineers, Expedition Doctors and Physiologists, sponsored by the Alpine Club (London) edited by Charles Clarke, Michael Ward and Edward Williams.

C H A P T E R   F I V E

The Mt. Whitney Trail

Pack it in. Pack it out.
There is no garbage service on the Mt. Whitney Trail.

The Forest Service trail from Whitney Portal provides a route that almost any healthy person can climb with little trouble. It is well-graded, almost too easy a grade for hikers in top physical shape. The few stream crossings are shallow and present no problem. The trail surface is rocky in some places, as little soil is to be found at these elevations. This only requires a little care in choosing a spot for your feet, and possibly a slower pace.

The biggest problem is the rapid change in elevation. In the Himalayas and elsewhere, climbers plan on moving up the peak at the rate of 1,000 feet per day, to allow for acclimatization. Here, many drive from near sea level to 8,300 feet, then immediately attempt to climb the remaining 6,000 feet. The mountain sickness (also known as altitude sickness) that may result is quite uncomfortable and in some cases can be dangerous. Mountain sickness can completely destroy the chances for a successful climb. While Whitney has been climbed in little over two and a half hours, with a round-trip of four hours and ten minutes, this is not a goal for most climbers. If you have not been climbing at high elevations for the past several months, we recommend three full days for a pleasant trip. If possible, arrive at Whitney Portal in time to camp near there for at least one night before attempting the ascent. The time spent at the 8,300 foot level may mean the difference between a success and or miserable trip.

The next morning, make the leisurely climb to Trail Camp, passing Mirror Lake. Camping is not allowed here, but it is a pleasant lunch stop, and the break may make the 1,500 foot climb to Trail Crest a little

Mt. Whitney summit shelter in spring. Photo: R.J. Secor

easier. The following day, by arising early and getting on the trail by 6:00 am, an easy climb will put you on the summit by noon or shortly thereafter. The trip can be completed late that afternoon or the next day.

Getting there.

Mt. Whitney from Los Angeles

From Los Angeles take Interstate 5 north to Highway 14. Go north on Highway 14 through Palmdale and Lancaster, toward the desert community of Mojave. This is a good place to fill your car with gas and have a quick bite to eat. Continue north on Highway 14, passing through Red Rock State Park. Just west of Ridgecrest, Highway 14 merges with Highway 395. Continue on Highway 395 through Olancha. There are gas stations in Olancha and an eatery or two which serve up a good home-cooked meal. To the east of the highway is the vast dry bed of Owens Lake with the Inyo Mountains as a backdrop. On the east side of the lake is the small historic town of Keeler, where a steep, winding dirt road can be taken to the crest of the Inyo Mountains to the historic 19th century mining district of Cerro Gordo, now privately owned and actively mined from time to time. Back in the late 1800's, silver mined at Cerro Gordo was taken down to Keeler where boats would transport loads of the precious silver bars across Owens Lake to the bustling port town of Cartago, on the western shore. The ore would then be transported by wagon to Los Angeles, then shipped to San Francisco. An interesting side trip on your way up 395 is a visit to the historic adobe Cottonwood charcoal kilns, just north of Olancha (look for the historical marker on the right side of the highway) where, due to the proximity of trees in the Sierra Nevada, charcoal was made for use in the processing of silver at the mill site, the ruins of which are located just east of Keeler. North of Owens Lake is Lone Pine, gateway to Whitney Portal. Turn left on the Whitney Portal Road and drive approximately 13 miles west to the parking area.

Mt. Whitney from San Francisco

There are several different route options when driving from San Francisco. The most straightforward, is to head east on Interstate 80 toward Sacramento. East of Sacramento, continue on Interstate 80 to Highway 395 or take Highway 50 through South Lake Tahoe to Highway 395. Go south on 395 through the Nevada towns of Minden and Gardnerville, passing Topaz Lake. Continue south through Bridgeport, county seat of Mono County.

Approximately 6.3 miles south of Bridgeport is the turnoff for the historic mining town of Bodie, a nice side trip and well worth a visit. Founded in 1859, Bodie was one of the most prosperous mining towns in the west and today is the best preserved ghost town in California. The Bodie Road is closed to vehicles during winter, but makes a fine cross-country ski trip combined with an overnight snowcamp. South of the Bodie Road, is Conway Summit, highest point on Highway 395 between San Diego and the Canadian border. The view across Mono Lake and the Great Basin from this spot is spectacular at any time of the year. Guided tours of Mono Lake are given during the summer months, providing information on the natural and local history of the area. Continue south through Lee Vining, past Tioga Road, the eastern approach to Yosemite. Further south, pass the turnoffs for June Lake and Mammoth Mountain, the finest skiing in the eastern Sierra Nevada, on to Bishop, Big Pine, Independence (the county seat of Inyo County) to Lone Pine. Turn right on the Whitney Portal Road and drive 13 miles west to the parking area.

Parking

Parking is available at Whitney Portal trailhead for both day and overnight use. Backpackers must park in the overnight area. Overflow parking is on the south shoulder of the road, 500 feet east of the overnight area. Park in a designated area, clear of the roadway, securely setting your parking brake and blocking a wheel. Lock your vehicle and don't leave food or any scented items in your car. Bears live in the area and are in constant search of food.

Bears

Bear-resistant food canisters, small black containers that fit in or strap to a backpack, are now required for overnight trips on many Sierra trails including the Mt. Whitney Trail. The author hiked over Cottonwood Pass to Mt. Whitney and found that the canisters hold about six days worth of food, well-planned and tightly packed for two. Canisters can be purchased or rented from the USFS and various outdoor retailers. Bears know that it is a lot easier to feed themselves from improperly stored food, garbage or any kind of scented items left in a car, cooler, tent, or backpack than to forage in nature. Once a bear has obtained these items, it becomes dependent on human food sources, and as a result loses its inherent fear of people. Improper food storage has become a major problem in the backcountry and because of this, encounters with bears in popular backcountry campsites are common. Adult Black Bears *(Ursus americanus)* weigh up to 350 pounds and will do major damage. One fellow came back from a climb of Whitney to find that a bear had walked on the roof of his sports utility vehicle, ripping off a passenger door to get a package of cookies he had left *under* the car wrapped in a garbage bag topped with rocks. Had this fellow used the food storage boxes at the trailhead this incident would have been avoided. Recently, a sow (female bear) was killed because she had lost her inherent fear of humans. We are the only ones who can keep bears and other Sierra species wild and alive, beginning with proper food storage. Minimize the amount of food you bring to Whitney Portal before you arrive. Whenever you leave your vehicle, even if just for a few mintues,

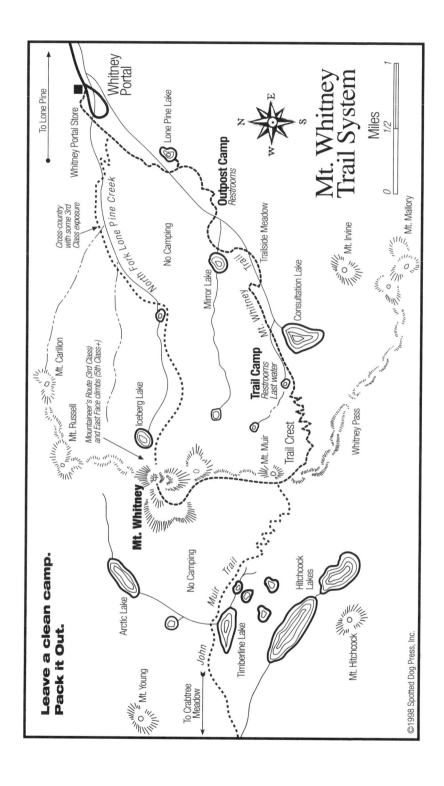

Mt. Whitney Trail System

Leave a clean camp. Pack it Out.

To Lone Pine

Whitney Portal

Whitney Portal Store

Lone Pine Lake

Outpost Camp
Restrooms

Trailside Meadow

Consultation Lake

Trail Camp
Restrooms
Last water

Mirror Lake

Mt. Whitney Trail

Cross-country
with some 3rd
Class exposure

North Fork Lone Pine Creek

Iceberg Lake

Mt. Carillon

Mt. Russell

Mountaineer's Route (3rd Class)
and East Face climbs (5th Class+)

No Camping

Mt. Whitney

Arctic Lake

No Camping

Muir Trail

John

Timberline Lake

Hitchcock Lakes

To Crabtree Meadow

Mt. Young

Mt. Hitchcock

Mt. Muir

Trail Crest

Whitney Pass

Mt. Irvine

Mt. Mallory

Miles
0   1/2   1

N W E S

©1998 Spotted Dog Press, Inc.

store all food and scented items in the food storage lockers at the trailhead.

If staying at campgrounds store all food, sealed drinks, coolers, water bottles, toiletries (toothpaste, soap, shampoo, deodorant) and scented items in the brown food storage boxes now located at most trailhead parking areas and campgrounds. For hikers going beyond Mt. Whitney to destinations in Sequoia/Kings Canyon National Park, food storage lockers have been placed in some of the more remote backcountry campsites.

Hiking the Mt. Whitney Trail

Suggested hiking maps: Mount Whitney, CA and Mt. Langley, CA USGS 7.5 minute topographic maps.

The mileages on the Mt. Whitney trail have been open to question. In preparation for the Mt. Whitney Marathon, Bob and Jerri Lee of Ridgecrest measured the distances from Whitney Portal to the summit, using a surveyor's tape. Their values are used here.

0.0 miles (8,361'): The trailhead is located just east of the Whitney Portal Store. A large wilderness display is located here, which is well worth studying. The trail starts immediately behind the display. The first half mile crosses treeless terrain and is often hot during summer months.

0.5 miles (8,480'): The trail enters John Muir Wilderness. Campfires are not allowed in the Whitney drainage. Carry portable backpacking stoves. The trail works back and forth, often in chaparral and may be quite warm on a summer's day. Near the top of the brushy area, about two miles from the starting point, a couple of small springs may be found running alongside the trail. Just before reaching the Lone Pine Lake junction, the trail fords the creek. A log bridge has been built over the creek.

2.5 miles (9,420'): Lone Pine Lake Junction. The left branch leads over a small rise to this beautiful lake. The main trail continues straight ahead, up a dry sandy streambed. A short series of switchbacks on the right wall crosses over a shoulder to Outpost Camp.

3.5 miles (10,365'): Outpost Camp. The newly rerouted trail no longer crosses through the meadow. It hugs some granite slabs on the south side of the meadow as you enter Outpost Camp from the south. This is a good campsite, but it is still a long way to the summit. Use the restrooms provided. A few more switchbacks, then another stream crossing and we are at Mirror Lake.

Summit sign. Photo: Pete Yamagata

4.0 miles (10,640′): Mirror Lake. This is a nice picnic area, but don't drink the water. Giardia Lamblia, a particularly nasty parasite, is endemic to the Sierra. The microscopic Giardia cysts can be removed from water most successfully with the use of a portable water filter. If you're backpacking Mt. Whitney, carry a water filter to conserve on weight. Carrying all the water you need for a few days plus a full pack might get a little heavy. If you're dayhiking it, you'll probably want to carry the water you'll need (approximately 3-4 quarts). Bringing water to a boil, or in a pinch, treating it with iodine crystals are other options.

Just past Mirror Lake, the trail turns left and, at the last stream crossing, is sometimes submerged. Follow the trail through the moist spots, then continue to your right.

5.0 miles (11,395′): Trailside Meadows. The trail now climbs to the right and continues up to a ridge, contouring over a bench to Trail Camp.

6.0 miles (12,039′): Trail Camp. This group of little ponds is the last sure water. On the north side of the larger pond is a sandy area with several large rocks. This area provides good campsites with some wind protection and is recommended for overnight camp. Use the restrooms provided. In case of a storm, it is possible to seek shelter under the larger rocks. The next two miles, with its 97 switchbacks, leads to Trail Crest.

8.2 miles (13,000'): Trail Crest. This is where the summit ridge is crossed to the western slope. Here, the trail enters Sequoia National Park and remains in the park to the summit of Mt. Whitney. Dogs and firearms are not permitted past this point. The true Whitney Pass is about a mile south and is seldom used. From here the trail drops slightly to meet the John Muir Trail.

8.7 miles (13,480'): The John Muir Trail. The route now passes the "windows," with their spectacular view of the Owens Valley, then continues on up to the summit plateau. Follow the trail as it winds its way across a few more switchbacks, passing the stone shelter to the broad summit of Mt. Whitney.

10.7 miles (14,496'): You made it! The summit of Mt. Whitney. Sign the register in the historic summit shelter and enjoy the view.

C H A P T E R   S I X

Reservations Are Required

Anyone planning to climb Mt. Whitney during the quota season, from May 15 through November 1, must reserve a permit for their trip from the Inyo National Forest Wilderness Reservation Office in Bishop, California. Though permits are required year-round for all overnight trips and dayhikes past Lone Pine Lake, 2.8 miles from Whitney Portal Trailhead, the quota season is the most popular time of the year to climb Mt. Whitney. In an effort to minimize human impact to the fragile ecology of the Mt. Whitney Zone, which includes the Whitney Portal trailhead and the North Fork of Lone Pine Creek (Mountaineer's Route and East Face), a limited number of people are allowed on quota trails each day. During the summer, a climb of Mt. Whitney via the Whitney Portal Trailhead is not for those seeking a quiet wilderness experience. The current number of people allowed on the Mt. Whitney trail by permit per day is 150 for dayhikes and 50 for overnight trips (15 people per day on the North Fork). The process for obtaining a permit for Mt. Whitney has changed year to year as demand has grown. Permits for the main Mt. Whitney Trail are 100% reservable from May 15 through November 1, and are given out by lottery. The few permits that aren't reserved or are cancelled will be available on a walk-in basis starting at noon the day before your planned date of entry. North Fork Trail permits are 60% reservable with 40% available on a walk-in basis. Note: the Mt. Whitney Ranger Station will give North Fork users a *Nature Calls Kit,* that contains instructions and supplies for a 3-4 day trip per person. Used kits are deposited in the human waste receptacle at the Whitney Portal Trailhead (more about this on page 62).

How to Obtain a Permit

Information for the Mt. Whitney and other Inyo National Forest trails, including the application for the Mt. Whitney Trail, can be obtained by calling the Inyo National Forest at (760)873-2485. The application form can also be downloaded from the Inyo National Forest website:

www.r5.fs.fed.us/inyo which provides information on a variety of subjects including permits and current conditions. When you reserve your permit you will be asked for alternate dates and trailheads (more alternate dates, the better chance of getting a permit), order of preference, and the number of people in your party. The maximum group size on a permit is 15 people.

Submit the application by <u>mail or fax only</u> to the Inyo National Forest Wilderness Reservation Office during the month of February for all entry dates during the quota season. Processing begins mid-February, so it is advantageous to get your request in early in the month. Include the fee for the Mt. Whitney Zone, currently $15.00 per person (subject to change, and non-refundable if your reservation is confirmed). Duplicate applications will be double-charged. Mail your application with the correct fee payment (check or money order made payable to *USDA Forest Service*) to: Wilderness Reservations Office, Inyo National Forest, 873 N. Main Street, Bishop CA 93514, or FAX your application (with credit card information, VISA or MasterCard only) to (760)873-2484. When you do succeed in getting a reservation, you will receive an information packet from the Inyo National Forest called *Hiking the Whitney Trail* that should answer any questions.

The reservation fee is applicable to those hiking into the Mt. Whitney Zone via the Pacific Crest, John Muir or High Sierra Trails. The Mt. Whitney Zone boundaries are to the east, just above Lone Pine Lake; to the west, just above Crabtree Ranger Station, but below Timberline Lake; to the north along the boundary between Sequoia National Park and Inyo National Forest, just below Tulainyo Lake and including the North Fork of Lone Pine Creek; and to the south along Whitney Pass to Discovery Pinnacle following the ridge to the east. Wilderness permits for backpackers entering from trails on the west side of Sequoia and Kings Canyon National Parks can be obtained from the appropriate National Park Service station. Currently a $10 flat fee applies to permits issued from trailheads on the west side at Sequoia and Kings Canyon National Parks. Wilderness permits are required for all overnight travel in the Sierra Nevada. On popular trails during the quota season, you have a much better chance of getting a permit if you plan on starting your trip between Sunday and Thursday. Fridays, Saturdays and holidays are the busiest.

C H A P T E R   S E V E N

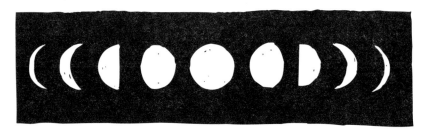

Moonlight Ascent

An increasing number of climbers are finding that a moonlight ascent of Mt. Whitney is an unique and enjoyable way of reaching the summit. Since this is a one-day, or rather a one-night climb, it is not recommended for those not in top physical condition. For those who are, the views of the world by moonlight, the coolness, and lack of sunglare may make this a highly recommended way to hike Mt. Whitney.

Choose a night, just a few nights after a full moon (consult your calender). This will insure the moonlight falling on the eastern slopes while you are climbing there. The moon will then cross the crest with you and provide light on the western slope.

Sierra nights can be cold, especially with a brisk wind. Carry a parka, sweater, a warm wool hat and warm gloves. A lightweight bivy sack, can make any evening on Whitney's summit all the more enjoyable. If you reach the summit before sunrise, the wait can be cold. Carry a flashlight or headlamp (you may not need it with the moonlight), lunch, trail snacks and at least two quarts of water. Sunrise pictures are something special. An overnight permit with a Mt. Whitney Zone Stamp is required for all moonlight hikes, with or without camping. No excuses! Park in the overnight parking area.

Whitney on the Web

The Inyo National Forest and the National Park Service have their own web sites with current, detailed information on obtaining a permit for any hike in the Mt Whitney Zone. However, reservations for permits must still be obtained through traditional means — by phone, fax, or mail. Web addresses, like permit regulations, are apt to change now and then. The most recent web addresses for Mt. Whitney information are listed below.

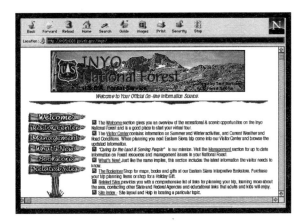

Whitney Web Addresses

Inyo National Forest/Mt. Whitney:
www.r5.fs.fed.us/inyo

Mt. Whitney information:
www.nps.gov/seki/whitney.htm

Sequoia and Kings Canyon Virtual Visitor Center
Information on Mt. Whitney from the west and east
www.nps.gov/seki/mainvc.htm

C H A P T E R E I G H T

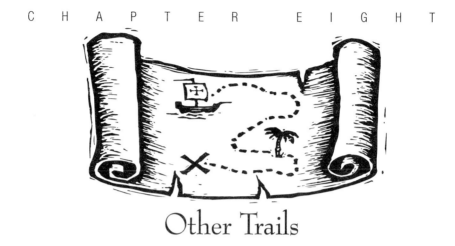

Other Trails

Hikers who enjoy long cross-country treks, often climb Mt. Whitney by several alternate routes. Those who enjoy employing pack stock will likewise enjoy exploring more of the Sierra than can be seen in a dash from Lone Pine. Permits are required for all overnight hikes in Sequoia National Park. Reserve your permit no later than three weeks before the start of your trip.

Giant Forest

Perhaps the most popular alternate trip to Mt. Whitney is the Trans-Sierra jaunt from Giant Forest, completely across the Sierra Nevada, ending at Lone Pine. While this is often referred to as a 100-mile hike, if car transportation can be arranged from the trail end to Lone Pine, the distance is about 80 miles. This trip is for experienced hikers with good physical endurance. A permit, available from the Lodgepole Visitor Center, is required for all overnight stays in Sequoia National Park. From Crescent Meadows, the High Sierra Trail hugs the 7,000-foot contour to Bearpaw Meadows (lodging and meals available during the season). From Bearpaw Meadows, a new section of trail climbs past Hamilton Lakes with its spectacular view of Eagle Scout Peak and passes over the Kaweah Gap. It then descends the Big Arroyo to the Kern River. The trail swings north, leaving the river at Junction Meadow and joining the John Muir Trail at Wallace Creek. This is followed past Crabtree Meadow (last campsite below the peak), and joins the Mt. Whitney near Trail Crest, two miles south of the summit of Mt. Whitney. Hang food away from camp, 24-hours a day, to keep the bears from coming into your camp. The Forest Service has placed food storage boxes (FSB) to be used by hikers at the following locations:

	Elevation	Distance from point above	Distance from Crescent Meadow	Distance from Mt. Whitney	
Crescent Meadow	6,800'	0.0	0.0	68.5	
Bearpaw Meadow	7,760'	11.4	11.4	57.1	FSB
Hamilton Lakes	8,235'	4.6	16.0	52.5	FSB
Kaweah Gap	10,400'	5.5	21.5	47.0	
Upper Funston Mdw	6,720'	20.0	41.5	27.0	FSB
Junction Meadow	8,036'	11.5	53.0	15.5	FSB
Wallace Creek	10,400'	4.0	57.0	11.5	
Crabtree Meadow	10,329'	3.0	60.0	8.5	FSB
Mt. Whitney	14,496'	8.5	68.5	0.0	

Mineral King

From the alpine-like village of Mineral King several routes are available. The most popular leads over Franklin Pass, down Rattlesnake Creek, reaching the Kern River, a little south of the High Sierra Trail. From this junction, the route is the same as the above route. A much rougher but shorter route climbs directly east from Mineral King over Sawtooth Pass, dropping past Columbine Lake to the Big Arroyo. This trail is often in poor shape and is not recommended for pack stock. A third trail leads over Timber Gap, then cuts back and up over the hot, dusty Black Rock Pass and down again to the High Sierra Trail in the Big Arroyo.

	Elevation	Distance from point above	Distance from Mineral King	Distance from Mt. Whitney	
Mineral King	7,830'	0.0	0.0	52.1	
Franklin Lakes	10,240'	3.6	3.6	48.5	
Franklin Pass	11,680'	1.5	5.1	47.0	
Kern River	6,585'	16.0	21.1	31.0	
Upper Funston Mdw	6,720'	4.0	25.1	21.0	FSB
Junction Meadow	8,036'	11.5	36.6	15.5	FSB
Crabtree Meadow	10,329'	7.0	43.6	8.5	FSB
Mt. Whitney	14,496'	8.5	52.1	0.0	

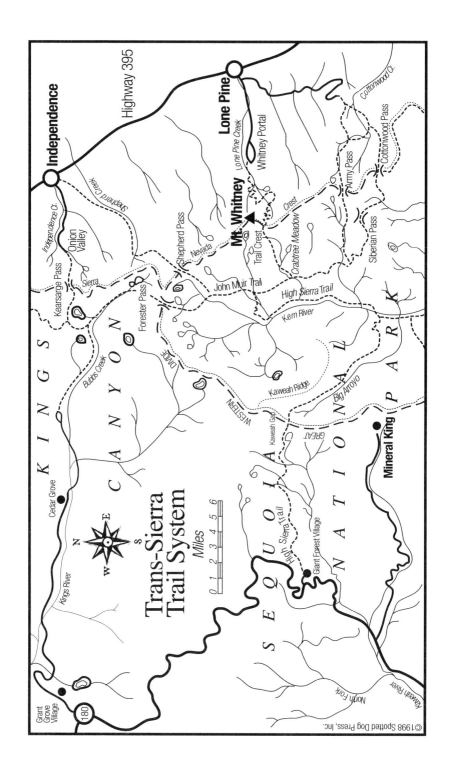

Trans-Sierra
Trail System

Miles

0 1 2 3 4 5 6

Highway 395

Independence

Lone Pine

Mt. Whitney

Lone Pine Creek

Whitney Portal

Cottonwood Cr.

Cottonwood Pass

Army Pass

Crest

Siberian Pass

Crabtree Meadow

Trail Crest

Nevada

Shepherd Pass

Shepherd Creek

Independence Cr.

Onion Valley

Kearsarge Pass

Sierra

Forester Pass

John Muir Trail

High Sierra Trail

Kern River

DIVIDE

Bubbs Creek

K I N G S

C A N Y O N

Kaweah Ridge

WESTERN

Big Arroyo

GREAT

N A T I O N A L   P A R K

Kaweah Gap

S E Q U O I A

High Sierra Trail

Mineral King

Cedar Grove

Kings River

Giant Forest Village

Grant
Grove
Village

180

North Fork

Kaweah River

Cedar Grove

A less commonly used route starts from the roadend above Cedar Grove in Kings Canyon and works its way up to Bubbs Creek, joining the John Muir Trail, just south of the trail junction from Kearsarge Pass. A loop trip can be arranged, returning to Giant Forest.

	Elevation	Distance from point above	Distance from Cedar Grove roadend	Distance from Mt. Whitney	
Roadend	4,855'	0.0	0.0	49.5	
Bubbs Creek	5,098'	5.0	5.0	44.5	
Junction Meadow	8,080'	9.5	14.5	35.0	FSB
Vidette Meadow	9,600'	2.5	17.0	32.5	FSB
Forester Pass	13,120'	7.0	24.0	25.5	
Wallace Creek	10,400'	10.0	34.0	15.5	FSB
Crabtree Meadow	10,329'	7.0	41.0	8.5	FSB
Mt. Whitney	14,496'	8.5	49.5	0.0	

Onion Valley

Two longer trips may be taken from Onion Valley (9,120'), west of Independence, once home of California pioneer writer Mary Austin (*Land of Little Rain*). It is about four miles to Kearsarge Pass from the beginning of the Onion Valley Trailhead. A short drop leads to Charlotte Lake, a suitable campsite (Bullfrog Lake is closed). This short climb over the pass is an excellent first day conditioner. From here the trail leads up over Forester Pass and joins the above route at Tyndall Creek Junction, but starts lower by some 3,000 feet.

	Elevation	Distance from point above	Distance from Onion Valley	Distance from Mt. Whitney	
Onion Valley	9,120'	0.0	0.0	35.7	
Kearsarge Pass	11,800'	4.0	4.0	31.7	
Bullfrog Lake	10,600'	2.0	6.0	29.7	
Forester Pass	13,120'	8.2	14.2	21.5	
Tyndall Creek Junction	10,880'	5.0	19.2	16.5	
Wallace Creek	10,400'	5.0	24.2	11.5	FSB
Crabtree Meadow	10,329'	3.0	27.2	8.5	FSB
Mt. Whitney	14,496'	8.5	35.7	0.0	

Horseshoe Meadow

Another less travelled route may be taken from the Horseshoe Meadow roadend up the Cottonwood Creek watershed, then over the New Army Pass to an intersection with the Pacific Crest Trail, which rims the Cottonwood Creek Basin, contouring from Mulkey Pass to Siberian Pass.

	Elevation	Distance from point above	Distance from Horseshoe Meadow roadend	Distance from Mt. Whitney	
Roadend	9,660'	0.0	0.0	30.7	
New Army Pass	12,385'	7.2	7.2	23.7	
Siberian Pass Trail	10,820'	7.0	14.2	16.5	
Crabtree Meadow	10,329'	8.0	22.2	8.5	FSB
Mt. Whitney	14,496'	8.5	30.7	0.0	

Hiking With Our Canine Friends

We love our canine friends, however, *they are not permitted* on the trails or in the backcountry of Sequoia or Kings Canyon National Parks, or on the summit of Mt. Whitney which is on the border of Sequoia National Park and Inyo National Forest. From the Mt. Whitney Trail, the cutoff for canines is at Trail Crest — no dogs allowed past this point.

There are plenty of places dogs are allowed, including most BLM, USFS lands (with the exception of certain research areas, such as the Bighorn Sheep Zoological Area near Mt. Williamson, and any other areas that may be designated off-limits for archeological or environmental reasons), and most USFS Wilderness Areas. Dogs are not allowed in the backcountry of National Parks, nor are they permitted in the backcountry or on the trails in California State Parks, though this rule sometimes varies. Dogs are allowed on leash in Bodie State Historic Site, but they are not allowed in San Jacinto State Park near Palm Springs. It is always best to check ahead with the managing park agency before traveling many miles with your dog, only to find out that canines are not allowed on the trail.

We would like to say a few words about taking dogs on trails. We know of someone who recently lost his dog near the Palisades Crest, west of Big Pine, California. "Mandy" was unleashed and wearing a dogpack.

For two weeks, Mandy's owner returned to the area to look for her. He notified local animal control, posted reward ads in the local newspaper, and signs in local neighborhoods, until business took him to Hong Kong. Nearly a month had passed, with no word about Mandy.

One morning, a homeowner in Big Pine walked out into her backyard and discovered an emaciated and very dehydrated dog playing with her own dog. It was Mandy. Though she had lost her pack and endured the backcountry for almost a month, she made it back to civilization. Dog and owner were happily reunited, but others have not been so lucky.

Nancy Smith of Inyo County Animal Control and Inyo County Search and Rescue recommends, as do we, that owners keep their dog leashed while hiking in the Sierra, especially if the dog is going to carry its own pack. There have been cases where dogs who have gotten away from their owners while carrying packs, have been found drowned in streams or have become hung up on trees or snags, unable to escape. A dog who is used to comfort of the house can become very easily disoriented in the backcountry.

A few other good reasons to keep your dog on a leash include: mountain lions; bears; pack animals; children and people who are afraid of dogs; people who don't like dogs; and dogs who run uncontrolled chasing the native wildlife. Carry a leash with you at all times, and make sure your dog has an ID on it's collar. By keeping your dog leashed and close to you, you can assure your pet's safety and happiness.

East Face of Mt. Whitney. Photo: Gary Vallé

C　H　A　P　T　E　R　　　N　I　N　E

Technical Routes

A technical climb on rock or snow by a trained, skilled mountaineer in the right state of mind using the right gear, is a safe and enjoyable venture. If any one of these elements is missing, it becomes an unsafe and an unjustified activity. Anyone who has not received technical climbing instruction or has not climbed with trained climbing groups should not attempt any of Mt. Whitney's East Face routes, with the possible exception of the Mountaineer's Route. Though not as technically difficult as routes on the East Face, the Mountaineer's Route poses its own challenges with a traverse across a short field of ice (depending on the snow year) and some exposed 3rd class climbing.

All routes up Mt. Whitney are physically demanding and anyone going for the summit should be prepared. Proper footwear, ropes and climbing hardware are necessary for these attempts. In general, a climbing party should consist of at least two ropes of two climbers, possibly climbing on alternate routes, or one rope or support party. Permits are required for all East Face climbs. Helmets are essential.

Unfortunately, this entire drainage has been so damaged by overuse, that the USFS is in the process of designating one standard route. Where there was once a lovely tarn located in the bowl where Clyde Meadows is found, there is only damaged vegetation, and footpaths going everywhere.

When improperly buried human feces became a significant problem in this drainage, the USFS successfully implemented the *Pack Out Your Poop* program. The Mt. Whitney Ranger Station provides each North Fork user with a "Nature Calls Kit" which includes instructions and supplies for a 3 to 4 day trip, per person. After the trip, deposit your full white bag in the human waste receptacle located at the Whitney Portal trailhead.

Approach

Just before the large stream crossing (the second creek), a half mile above the roadend at Whitney Portal, the North Fork Trail swings to the right, climbing slowly to where it meets the North Fork of Lone Pine Creek. At first, it is quite evident, but soon becomes less distinct. Approximately a half mile after leaving the junction, the route crosses the creek to south side. Proceed upstream on the south side watching the north side of the stream for a distinct, large pine tree that appears to be growing out of the rock. Directly below the pine tree is a brushy deciduous-looking tree. Cross the stream to the north side and head for these two trees. Climb up over the brushy tree. Behind this brushy tree, a little 10-12 foot chute appears, directly below the distinct pine tree. Climb up the chute. The roots of the pine can be used to pull yourself up, a "vegetable belay" of sorts. Just above the pine tree, the series of rock ledges known as the "Ebersbacher Ledges" appears. The route through them is obvious and is followed for a short half mile, across some airy third class. The north wall gradually becomes more gentle and rocky, with brushy slopes provide easier going. This continues to Lower Boy Scout Lake, which is nice place to camp. The lake is skirted south shore, and then continues on the south (left) side of the stream. Here, the trail is again quite evident, and passes through a stretch of timber. Another half mile, and the route steepens, where the surfaces are a mixture of gravel slopes, by which we gain some 1,000 feet of elevation. An area of talus brings us to Clyde Meadows. This area is often used as a base camp for Mt. Whitney's East Face climbs.

Beyond this point, cross to the left of the main stream and climb over large talus blocks. At the crest of this slope, recross to the north side. Water on the polished rock may freeze in cold weather and will demand extreme caution. Since this is more strenuous and the icy section is safe for careful climbers, the choice of a route becomes a matter of individual judgment.

At the top of this slope, the grade lessens and there is scattered brush and White Bark Pine. A slope of large broken talus leads from here to the area below the great East Face of Mt. Whitney. Swinging to the right, work past a waterfall to the bench on which Iceberg Lake is located. Most climbers camp here. No wood fires are permitted. It is recommended that a climbing helmet be worn on all technical climbs.

Rating the Climbs

The standard system for rating the difficulty of mountain climbs is called the Yosemite Decimal System. It was introduced by the Sierra Club in 1937 and is still in use today, though the descriptions of 5th and 6th Class have been modified. The system is a general guide to help determine the difficulty of each climb. Each person will have to be the final judge of their own ability on any route. The ratings are as follows:

Class 1: Trail walking. The Mt. Whitney Trail is an excellent example of a Class 1 route.

Class 2: Includes more rugged terrain, like scree (loose, sandy rock) or talus (larger rocks and boulders) where the hands and feet must be used for balance.

Class 3: Terrain becomes steeper as boulders and other obstacles are encountered. Arms and legs are used for climbing, not just balancing. Handholds are usually easily identified. There is increased exposure, meaning there is a risk of falling or being injured. People who have hiked mostly on trails might feel initially uncomfortable with Class 3 and may want someone to belay them with a climbing rope across certain third-class sections.

Class 4: Terrain is steep and exposed. Most people require the use of a rope for protection. A degree of skill and a thorough knowledge of climbing procedure, including belaying for safety, is necessary. Handholds are less defined and the risk of falling is greatly increased. Also increased, is the possibility of being injured by loose, falling or collapsing rock (rock that literally gives way beneath your feet). Many fourth-class Sierra climbs are very crumbly and the sound of falling rocks can be heard

The following pages show technical routes up the East Face of Mt. Whitney.
Page 64 shows the view from the southwest. Page 65 shows the view from the northeast.
The East Face should only be attempted by trained climbers. Photos: Pete Yamagata

Southeast Face Route

East Buttress (direct route)

Grand Staircase

Mountaineer's Route

Fresh Air Traverse

The Washboard

throughout the duration of the climb. Wearing a helmet is recommended.

Class 5: This is bonafide rock-climbing, requiring complete climbing equipment — ropes, seat harnesses, runners, helmets, and assorted hardware. It also requires a depth of experience, skill and knowledge of climbing procedure to assure a safe and enjoyable climb, free from injury.

Fifth-class climbs have their own unique ratings categories based on difficulty, beginning with 5 (the least difficult) up to 5.14 (the most difficult) with an additional alphabetized subcategorical listing (A1–A5) referencing the amount of additional aid, including anything from a ladder to an unusual or elaborate arrangement of hardware, needed to complete the climb. Simple rope work and standard usage of climbing hardware just won't cut it.

Class 6 (now A1–A5): The Class 6 rating category has essentially been replaced by the more modern A1–A5 rating. However, many climbing guides still refer to certain routes as Class 6.

Technical Climbs

Mountaineer's Route (Class 2 with one class 3 pitch): First ascent credited to John Muir, October 21, 1873. Between the north arete and the Great Buttress is a large couloir. The fan of scree extends to Iceberg Lake (12,640' – also known as East Face Lake on some maps). The most direct route bypasses the lake to the west, directly ascending the slope. This ample couloir is surfaced with talus and scree. Usually, some snow is found in this shady couloir, and if it presents any difficulty, keep to the left (south). This couloir is followed all the way to a notch on the ridge, separating the northern arete from the summit block. A short distance beyond this notch, go left directly up 400 to 500 feet over large steep blocks to the crest. Just before the summit is reached some 200 yards to the southeast, depending on the snow year, there is a short stretch of ice which has required the use of crampons and ice axe to cross. This is one of the most dangerous sections on the route, and has claimed several lives. Wearing a helmet on the Mountaineer's Route is recommended.

East Buttress (Class 5.6): First ascent by Robert Brinton, Glen Dawson, Muir Dawson, Richard Jones and Howard Koster, September 5, 1937. Bypass Iceberg Lake, climbing to the fan to the left of the Mountaineer's Route for some 500 feet, to a notch between the First Tower and Second Tower. Rope up here, and work up the east face of the Second Tower,

The Washboard. Photo: Murray Zichlinsky

turning right (north) approximately 15 feet below its summit, where a second notch is reached. Climb the first pitch above the notch with care. Follow the crest of the east buttress, up to a point just below the "Peewee," a massive, protruding block which seems to cling precariously to the side of the mountain. Go around Peewee on the right. A number of alternate routes over huge steps now present themselves, and the summit is easily reached.

Due to its exposed location, the climb can be quite free from snow, even in midwinter. Accordingly, the difficulty under these conditions can be substantially less than would be encountered on the East Face Route. The East Buttress climb has been clocked at 3.5 hours from Iceberg Lake, but most parties should plan on a full day. Helmets are essential.

East Face Route (Class 5.4 to 5.8 depending on variation): First ascent was by Norman Clyde, Robert L.M. Underhill, Glen Dawson and Jules Eichorn on August 16, 1939. Follow the East Buttress Route to the notch connecting the First Tower with the Buttress. As before, rope up for the exposed *Tower Traverse* (5.3) which was first climbed by Jules Eichorn and

Cathy Reynolds and friend on the Tower Traverse. Photo: Murray Zichlinsky

Marjory Bridge in 1934. Traverse to the left (south) and up onto an exposed, outward sloping ledge, ascending steeply upward for approximately 25 feet to a shelf. Traverse across the shelf for another 25 feet to the base of a short crack, about 15 feet in height, in the face of the wall. Climb to the top of this crack to the beginning of the Washboard, a third-class series of rippled scree-covered ledges. Climb the Washboard, which deadends against the face. Swing left, up and over a rib, then drop down some 30 feet onto a wide ledge. This is followed to a fold between the Buttress and the face. Twenty-five feet above this, there is a choice of several routes and variations. The main three routes are:

Fresh Air Traverse (Class 5.4): Traverse left onto the exposed face. Work up a shattered chimney. At the head of this, work right to the foot of the Grand Staircase, a series of eight or ten foot ledges.

Shaky Leg Crack (Class 5.7): Climbed by Morgan Harris, James N. Smith and Neil Ruge, June 9, 1936. From the point where the Fresh Air Traverse turned left, continue straight up the face into Shaky Leg Crack. This is followed to the bottom of the Grand Staircase.

Direct Crack (Class 5.8): First ascent by John D. Mendenhall, July 4, 1953. This crack is the fold mentioned above, and is about forty feet south of the right hand cliffs. Four pitons have been used.

After any of these variations, climb the Grand Staircase, easy class 3, to a large crack at the left. Climb over any of a series of blocks and sloping ledges, directly to the summit. WARNING: Summit visitors are inclined to throw rocks, cans or bottles from the top, presenting an added hazard.

Southeast Face (Class 5): First ascent October 11, 1941, by John and Ruth Mendenhall. North of the Whitney-Keeler Couloir is a buttress topped by a gendarme. This buttress is separated from the face by an overhanging chimney. Climb the buttress, Class 4, to where it is possible to cross to the chimney, above the overhang. This route is over loose rotten rock, and much of the difficulty is due to this formation. Continuous Class 4 climbing leads to the summit. A helmet is highly recommended, as small rocks are continually falling down this chimney.

C H A P T E R   N I N E

Up the East Face
By Norman Clyde

Among mountaineers, second in fascination to the making of first ascents is the finding of new routes up mountains already climbed, especially if these are difficult. As opportunities of accomplishing the former gradually diminish, climbers turn their attention to the discovery of new and more arduous ways of obtaining summits of mountains. Walking or riding being a rather tame mode of reaching them, in their estimations, they are forever seeking new problems of ascent which they may match their skill and strength, puny as these may be, compared with the forces of lofty mountains.

Scalable with comparative ease from the south, west and north, Mt. Whitney, the highest peak in the United States, has lured mountaineers in the quest of a "real climb." Last season a fairly difficult one was found going from the east up a broad chute culminating in a notch on an arete running northward from the peak and giving access to the north face which was followed to the summit. Unsatisfied with the discovery, however they began to consider whether the apparent sheer east face of Mt. Whitney might not be scaled.

It was with this object in view that a party of five motored westward from Lone Pine toward the base of the Sierra Nevada during the forenoon of August 15 of the present year. The group was one of proven climbing ability. It consisted of Dr. Underhill of Harvard University, one of the most expert rockclimbers in the United States; Francis Farquhar of San Francisco, prominent in the activities of the Sierra Club; Jules Eichorn from the same city and Glen Dawson from Los Angeles, both youths, but very skillful in rockclimbing; and the writer

of this sketch. It is pertinent too, that the first descent of the new route
was made by three Los Angeles youths: Walter Brem, Richard Jones
and Glen Dawson, on September 6, 1931.

Having arrived at the end of the road, some eight miles west of Lone
Pine, we transferred our baggage from automobiles to the backs of
several mules. After a short trudge up the sun-steeped eastern slope
of the range we swung around a shoulder and entered the refreshing
coolness and shade of Lone Pine Canyon with the summit of Mt. Whitney
looking from its head a few miles directly to the west. Charmed by the
alluring seclusion of the gorge with floor shaded by pine and fir; with
brook resounding through a canopy of birch and willow, with walls of
mellow-hued and pleasingly sculpted granite, we leisurely followed
the trail to Hunter's Flat, a distance of about four miles, and continued
up switchbacks to the south of it to an elevation of some 9,000 feet above
sea level. There the packs were removed from the mules.

After eating luncheon, we fitted our packs on our backs and, aban-
doning the trail began to pick our way up the North Fork of Lone Pine
Creek. Within a few hundred feet we came upon a projecting buttress
around which we swung, and began to scramble over broken rocks in
the direction of a crevice leading up a steeply-shelving granite slope
to a ledge running along the south wall of the gorge. Occasionally we
stopped to regale ourselves in the luscious wild currants which grew
abundantly among the chaotic talus through which we were passing.
Below as the stream bounded along sonorously, hidden from view by
a dense growth of birch and maple.

Upon arriving at the foot of the crevice, we scrambled up it as
best we could, laden with heavy and bulky packs, to a ledge which we
followed around a projection. Although the ledge shelved down to a
cliff, we strode rapidly along it in our rubber soled shoes, pausing now
and then to look down to the floor of the canyon several hundred
feet below us, or turning about to gaze eastward through its u-shaped
opening and across the wide basin of Owens Valley to the Inyo Mountains
— richly colored, glowing in the afternoon sunshine, and with a mass
of snowy-white cumulus clouds hovering above them. A scattering
of limber pines grew along the lower portion of the shelf and as it gradually ascended, considerable numbers of the foxtail variety began to
appear. To our left, a vertical wall of granite rose in places to a height
of several hundred feet.

Having reached the upper end of the shelf, we crossed a strip of talus to the border of a glacially-formed basin in which grew a beautiful grove of foxtail pines. Through these we filed along to the margin of a meadow at an altitude of some 10,000 feet. It was a fascinating spot, by craggy peaks and to the west of the great pinnacles and steep walls of Mt. Whitney. Being without a trail and difficult of access, seldom has human foot trodden its secluded recess, although but a few miles from Owens Valley. Presently, the sun sank behind the serrated peaks of Mt. Whitney, suffusing a few clouds that wreathed about their summits, with vivid-hued light.

The ensuing dawn was literally "rosy-fingered," the peaks of Mt. Whitney and those on either side of the cirques glowing in roseate light of marvelous beauty. After a hasty breakfast, we were soon on our way northward across the meadow hoary with frost, to the base of a slope which we ascended to a cleft in the rock up which we scrambled to an apron-like slope of glaciated granite. Across this we picked our way along a series of cracks to a grove of foxtail pine in another basin.

With this behind us, we clambered up the point of a long promontory extending eastward from a shallow basin directly to the east of Mt. Whitney. Along its narrow crest, we sped nimbly to the margin of the upper basin when we halted for a few minutes in order to survey the face of Mt. Whitney, but being able to make little of it, we walked northwestward a few hundred feet to a small lake which afforded a more satisfactory view. After careful scrutiny, a possible route was discovered. At best, however, it would be obviously a difficult one and any one of a number of apparent "gaps" in it might render it impracticable.

Up a steep acclivity sufficiently broken to permit easy progress we steadily climbed to the notch and there were roped up. Dr. Underhill and Glen Dawson were on one rope; Jules Eichorn and myself on the other. The first rope preceded along the shelf, but as feared, it suddenly terminated in a sheer wall. Upon hearing this, the second rope began to scale the face of the gendarme, but this proving rather hazardous, we swung to the right and succeeded in finding a narrow shelf, or rather the edge of an upright rock slab with a crevice behind it, along which we made our way to a notch behind the pinnacle. From this, we descended a few feet, rounded a protruding buttress on narrow ledges, and began to ascend a chute, rather steep but with surface sufficiently roughened to afford good footing.

After an ascent of a few hundred feet we entered an alcove-like recess where further direct advance was barred by a perpendicular wall. There we awaited rope number one which presently arrived and after a short pause climbed over a low ridge into another chimney, rope number two following. Both ropes then clambered up an overhang to a platform. From this, however, progress upward could be made only by climbing a steep and rather precarious crack. Rather than run the risk of a fall we decided to attempt a traverse around a buttress to the left to a slabby chimney beyond it.

As I swung out over the wall below the platform, an apparently firm rock gave way beneath my foot and went crashing down the sheer cliffs directly below, but as no one was in its path and my handholds were good, no harm resulted.

Rope number one then went around the buttress to reconnoiter and after a pause of some time, the other followed. The traverse proved to be one requiring considerable steadiness, as these ledges were narrow and there was a thousand feet of nothing below them. As we came around the projection we were confronted by a gap in a ledge with a narrow platform about eight feet below. There was the alternative of stepping across it — as far as a man of medium height could possibly reach, availing himself of rather poor handholds — or dropping down to the platform and climbing the other side of the gap. Some of the members of the party chose one method; some the other.

Once over the break in the ledge, we were obliged to pull ourselves over a rounded rock by clinging to a diagonal crack with our hands while our feet momentarily swung out over the thousand-foot precipice. We attacked a precipitous, slabby wall availing ourselves of narrow ledges for hand and footholds. A few rods of this, however, brought us to a rounded shoulder with a broad couloir above it.

After halting a short time for luncheon, we proceeded up the chimney, zigzagging back and forth as we clambered over and around great granite steps until we were confronted at the upper end of the chimney by a vertical wall about thirty feet in height. At one side of it, however, there was a narrow crevice up which one might scramble. After removing our rucksacks, we squirmed and corkscrewed up it, the last man tying the knapsacks to the rope carried by the first.

Above the couloir, somewhat to our surprise, we encountered rather easy climbing. We therefore unroped and began to ascend to the right toward the summit of Mt. Whitney. Within a few minutes we came within sight of a cairn a little more than two hundred feet above us.

Quickening the speed, we clambered hastily upward, arriving at the summit, considerably elated by the successful accomplishment of the first ascent of Mt. Whitney up its apparently unscalable eastern face. Francis Farquhar, having ascended the mountain by another route, was there to meet us.

After spending an hour or more on the top of Mt. Whitney, the party separated, three following the trail southward in order to ascend Mt. Muir, while Dr. Underhill and myself proceeded to descend the north face to a notch a few hundred feet below the summit. It was an easy descent along a rocky rib and down a wide chute to the right of it.

After an evening spent consuming enormous quantities of food and lounging about a campfire, we retired to our sleeping bags under nearby foxtail pines solemnly silent beneath a sky spangled with innumerable stars over-arching the mountains that loomed darkly around the basin. On the following morning we made up our packs and proceeded down the canyon, pleased at having added another outstanding climb to the already discovered number in the Sierra Nevada.

Norman Clyde is legendary in the history of Sierra Nevada mountaineering. With first ascents in the Sierra Nevada numbering in the thousands, he made more of them than anyone, climbing at a time when the equipment was primitive and access to the mountains difficult. Clyde climbed Mt. Whitney more than fifty times from every conceivable route. His book, *Close Ups of the High Sierra* is published by Spotted Dog Press, Inc.

A d d i t i o n a l   R e a d i n g

Brewer, William H., *Up and Down California in 1860-1864*, Edited by Francis Farquhar, University of California Press, Berkeley, CA 1966

Brown, Vinson, *The Sierra Nevadan Wildlife Region*, Naturegraph, Co., San Martin, CA 1954

Chalfant, William A., *The Story of Inyo*, Chalfant Press, Bishop, CA 1933

Clyde, Norman, *Close Ups of the High Sierra*, Spotted Dog Press, Inc. 1998

Farquhar, Francis, *History of the Sierra Nevada*, University of California Press in collaboration with Sierra Club, Berkeley, CA 1966

Fiero, Bill, *Geology of the Great Basin*, The University of Nevada Press, Reno, NV, 1986

Friends of the Eastern California Museum, *Mountains to the Desert, Selected Inyo Readings*, Eastern California Museum, Independence, CA 1988

King, Clarence, *Mountaineering in the Sierra Nevada*, University of Nebraska Press, Lincoln NE 1970

Knopf, Adolph, *A Geological Reconnaissance of the Inyo Range and the Eastern Slope of the Southern Sierra*, Government Printing Office, Washington, D.C. 1918

Matthes, Francois E., *Sequoia National Park – A Geological Album*, University of California Press, Berkeley, CA 1956

Munz, Philip and Keck, David, *A California Flora*, University of California Press, Berkeley, CA 1959

Norris, Robert N. and Webb, Robert W., *Geology of California*, John Wiley & Sons, NY 1976

Peters, Ed, *Mountaineering Freedom of the Hills*, The Mountaineers, Seattle, WA 1982

Schoenherr, Alan A., *A Natural History of California*, University of California Press, Berkeley, CA 1992

Secor, R.J., *The High Sierra Peaks, Passes and Trails*, The Mountaineers, Seattle, WA 1992

Smith, Genny Schumacher Smith, *Deepest Valley*, William Kaufmann Inc., Los Altos, CA 1972

Starr Jr., Walter, *Guide to the John Muir Trail and the High Sierra Region*, Sierra Club, San Francisco, CA 1974

Storer, Tracy I. and Usinger, Robert L., *Sierra Nevada Natural History*, University of California Press, Berkeley, CA 1973

Wheelock, Walt, Ropes, *Knots and Slings for Climbers*, La Siesta Press, Glendale, CA 1989

Whitney, J.D., Geology, Volume 1, *Geological Survey of California*, Caxton Press, Philadelphia, PA 1865

Voge, Hervey, editor, *A Climber's Guide to the High Sierra*, Sierra Club, San Francisco, CA 1962

Index

About the Authors

PHOTO: Randall Danta

Wynne Benti has hiked to Mt. Whitney in the Sierra Nevada, including more than four hundred mountains in the Mojave, Sonoran, and Great Basin deserts of the western United States, and Mexico, and Japan. A graduate of the University of California at Davis, Wynne published the Leaders Reference Book for the Leadership Training Program of the Sierra Club's largest chapter. Partial to the sun and vast open terrain of the desert, she has climbed El Picacho del Diablo, Botella d'Azul, and Cerro Pescadores in Baja, Weaver's Needle in the Superstitions, Baboquivari in southern Arizona, and the Guardian Angels in Zion. She lives and works in the Owens Valley.

Walt Wheelock traveled the mountains of California and the west for more than sixty years. Though not a climber of hair-raising technical ascents, he guided parties safely up many peaks. Walt was the award-winning founder of the Mountain Rescue Committee of the Sierra Club's largest regional chapter and was a member of numerous historical societies and mountaineering organizations.

Order Form

Mail to:
Spotted Dog Press
P.O. Box 1721
Bishop CA 93515
760-872-1524

U.S. Checks or
Money Orders only.
Thank you!

WWW.SPOTTEDDOGPRESS.COM

Name:
Address:
City   State   Zip Code
Daytime Phone   Evening Phone

Title	Price	Quantity	Total
Close Ups of the High Sierra Clyde 176 pages. Norman Clyde was California's greatest mountaineer, making more than 1,000 first ascents in the Sierra Nevada at a time when hiking boots had hobnails and Model T's were in vogue. This volume contains never before published writings and photographs.	$14.95		
Climbing Mt. Whitney Benti/Wheelock 80 pages. Information on permits, route descriptions, how to hike Whitney as a dayhike, backpack, moonlight hike or rock climb. Everything you need to know to get to the top of the highest peak in the contiguous U.S.	8.95		
Death Valley to Yosemite: Frontier Mining Camps and Ghost Towns Belden/DeDecker 192 pages. The most complete work available today on the mining camps from the Mojave Desert to the High Sierra. Beautifully written by two exceptional authors with detailed maps showing locations.	14.95		
Desert Summits: A Climbing & Hiking Guide to California and Southern Nevada Zdon 418 pages. Definitive guide to the highpoints of California's and Southern Nevada's desert ranges from the Great Basin to the Mexican border.	19.95		
Favorite Dog Hikes in and Around Los Angeles Benti 112 pages. The best-selling trail guide to the canine-friendly trails of Los Angeles. With a pattern for making dog boots for hiking.	10.95		
Grand Canyon Treks Butchart 288 pages. Butchart walked, air mattressed and climbed more than 12,000 miles in the Grand Canyon backcountry and is considered the leading authority.	16.95		
Out From Las Vegas Lawlor 288 pages. Guide to more than sixty adventures within a day's drive of Las Vegas by newspaper and travel reporter, Las Vegas native, Florine Lawlor.	16.95		
The Secret Sierra Gilligan 288 pages. Author David Gilligan combines narrative with natural history to describe this rugged and extreme mountain world above treeline.	18.95		
	Subtotal		
UPS Shipping $3.00 for 1st book plus $0.25 for each additional			
CA residents please add 7.25% sales tax **7.25% CA Sales Tax**			
Make check or money order payable to: Spotted Dog Press Mail to: P.O. Box 1721, Bishop, CA 93515 Allow 1-2 weeks for delivery. U.S. checks or money order only.	**Total**		